Rookhope's Landscape Legacies

by
Peter Bowes
and
Thomas Wall

Number 1 of a series Published by
The North Pennines Heritage Trust

with assistance from
Wear Valley District Council

Northern Rock Building Society

WEAR VALLEY
DISTRICT COUNCIL

Countryside Commision

COUNTRYSIDE
COMMISSION

I.S.B.N. No. 0 9513535 2 7

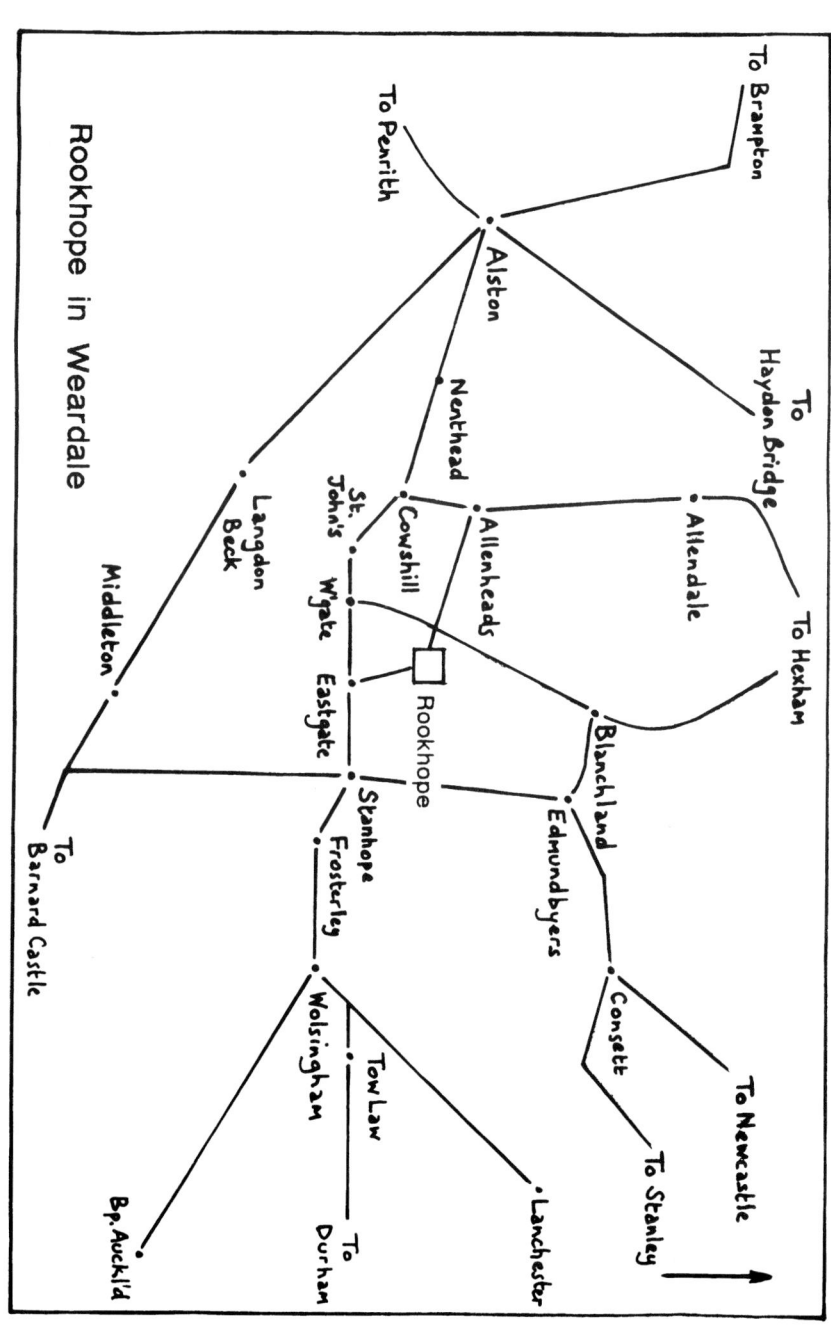

Rookhope in Weardale

To Brampton

To Penrith

Alston

To Hayden Bridge

Nenthead

St. John's

Cowshill

Allenheads

Allendale

To Hexham

Langdon Beck

W'gate

Rookhope

Blanchland

Middleton

Eastgate

Stanhope

Edmundbyers

To Barnard Castle

Frosterley

Tow Law

Consett

To Stanley

To Newcastle

Wolsingham

Lanchester

Bp.Auckl'd

To Durham

ROOKHOPE IN WEARDALE

Weardale has attracted more closely-spaced villages than any other North Pennine dale. With one exception, they are spread along the A689 road which follows the main valley floor. The one exception is Rookhope which lies hidden in the upper reaches of Rookhope Burn, to the north of the west-east line of settlements between Cowshill and Wolsingham.

A glance at the map might suggest the idea of isolation, a few miles by minor roads from each of Westgate, Eastgate and Allenheads, somewhat fanciful. The point to be stressed, though, is that for most of the time, movements in and out of the village are generated by the village itself. In short, Rookhope is off the beaten track.

Its remoteness has kept it small, different and currently in decline. Over the years, it has been inward-looking and a victim of its own short-lived and now disappeared economic success. It is very hard indeed to imagine Rookhope as a lively, noisy, bustling, energetic place with a population more than twice its present meagre 300. As you look around, it's scarcely credible that the village was self-sufficient with thriving churches and shops, crowded pubs and school, village activities requiring an institute and a Barrington Hall and, not least, cricket and football fields, tennis courts and bowling green.

But what defies belief more than anything is the time when farming in and around the village, the mining of lead, iron and fluorspar, lead-smelting and railways totally dominated people's lives with clockwork regularity, giving them a worthy reason for and no little pride in bringing up their families there. Those were the boom times, the glory days when the village supported a surgery, resident nurse, headmaster, vicar and policeman, ten shops and, for good measure, a private bus and taxi service.

In its heyday, Rookhope was the classic, industrial Company settlement, the best, by far, of its kind in the Dale. The Blackett Beaumont family firm, the Weardale Iron Company and, more recently the Weardale Lead Company have all stamped their imprint on the landscape, but, looking around, you might wonder *how* and *where*.

The four walks outlined below will answer these questions. However, there is a great deal more on the ground than industrial archaeology. There is, of course, the village itself - its site, shape, size and various component buildings - and the patterns of fields and stone walls around it. Rookhope may once have been an industrial village of some renown but over a longer period, agriculture has provided the continuity. That the two were able to coexist is not unusual in the northern dales. However, farming at Rookhope has also diminished dramatically. As you walk, its physical and economic problems are easily seen.

From almost any viewpoint, Rookhope's *site* on the floor of a narrow, steep-sided valley can be readily appreciated. However, careful observation shows that the village is not actually *on* the valley bottom. It is built mainly on a raised, drier shelf of land, slightly above river level, or on the lower slopes behind it. Immediately downstream from Rookhope, the advantages of this flatter terrace disappear into a river gorge where even modern building would prove very difficult.

In terms of houses and other buildings, the village is small, yet it straggles for 3/4 mile along the road from Stotfield Burn in the south to Burnside and Rookhope Nurseries in the west. Only at Boltsburn where the road crosses the Boltsburn tributary is there any clustering of dwellings and here is the heart of the village. Indeed, up to the present century, Rookhope was more commonly called Boltsburn.

Excepting Burnside which is a 20th-century addition, the entire settlement is on the north side of the river, facing south, at 1,040'-1,100' above sea level. That altitude tells us much about Rookhope's temperatures, length of growing season and the impossibility of arable farming - which brings us back to agriculture and the mediaeval origins of the village.

At some point in the mid-thirteenth century, the time had arrived for the Prince Bishop of Durham, the landlord of upper Weardale, to review his use of the great deer-hunting forest, part of which covered the Rookhope terrain. Clearing the forest for cattle-farming was the first priority. Almost certainly, extra wealth from the mining of lead was another. Establishing pioneer farms, however, provided guaranteed income whereas finding the lead veins, invisible at the surface, was slow and unpredictable.

No doubt the first stockmen were also charged with the search for lead deposits in stream beds near their farms. From these clues, the vital veins could then be traced upstream. It is probable, then, that the origins of the well-known dual economy were there from the beginning. The emphasis lay with farming first and mining second.

Where were the first farmer-miner holdings at Rookhope? The simplified map shows their probable location in 1300. It should be remembered that animal farming required sizeable areas of *improved* land, especially *meadow* (for winter hay) and *pasture* (summer grazing). Starting from scratch, as it were, the heavy work of felling trees, removing large stones from the soil and enclosing the land with walls would take both time and much communal effort.

Initially, then, the Rookhope farms were summer shielings or shields. During the summer season, when their animals could graze on open, rough ground, stock farmers were employed to build the stone walls illustrated on the map. The lines are *head dykes* marking the limits of meadows and pastures. The distribution of the early shielings and the arrangement of the different land uses are clearly shown.

Once completed, each of the five farms had quick and convenient access to *improved* hay land, *improved* grazing land and *unimproved* fell, providing stone, peat, timber, game, heather thatch, open grazing and, hopefully, lead ore or galena.

Another feature of farming at this time was the *communal* nature of cattle-rearing, not only in land clearance but also in matters of farming practice. See, for instance, how Redburn and Boltsburn farmers would *share* meadow and pasture; likewise with Boltsburn and Stotfield. Smaller Lintzgarth and Bolts Walls worked more independently. One more thing stands out: each farm dwelling stands next to a *tributary* stream supplying clean water and necessitating a short bridging-point.

A modern indication that the limits of pioneer farming up the Rookhope valley had been reached is the presence of heather and grass moor, west of Redburn and Lintzgarth. East of the Lintzgarth farmland, the fell also sweeps down to the Rookhope Burn creating a long expanse of open land. That land, as it happened, later proved to be the most valuable space for the village's industrial and railway developments.

Today's village is adjusting uncomfortably to change. Very limited local employment has taken a heavy toll on self-confidence. Where is the way forward? The old days now seem an age away. Industrial and agricultural prosperity has receded almost uncontrollably. Relics and memorials survive by chance. Property for sale, crumbling, or demolished says it all. Daily commuting and retirement homes have prevented further decline and, indeed, have brought in some new families. But local jobs and security are the root of the problem.

For reasons which are not altogether welcome, then, Rookhope is now a quiet, tranquil place. As you walk, enjoy the peace but let your mind and eyes take you to the prosperous days of a hardworking, closely-knit community, memories of which are fading fast.

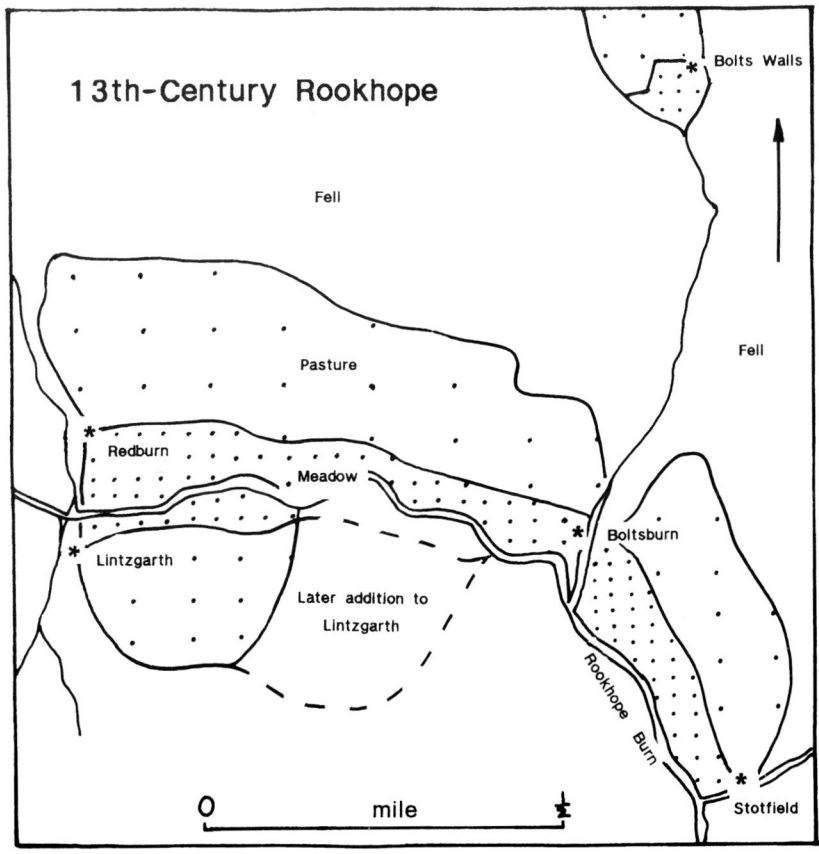

5

THE ROOKHOPE TRAILS

Four walks are described and explained in this booklet. The emphasis is very much on what exists now or did earlier in the present century. *EXPLANATION is* an important part of the presentation and closely complements *DESCRIPTION* of each route. The centre pages' map shows their location and length. Points of interest are marked on each separate route map by small dots, some are numbered and all are italicised in the text. Waymarkers should be visible along the walks.

All of the walks begin at the village hall car park in Boltsburn. THIS IS THE BEST PLACE TO PARK. It is situated just a few yards off the main road and next to the grey, flat-roofed village hall. A second parking area is also shown on the centre map, about a mile further west near the ruined smelt-mill arch. Here is an unsigned lay-by, immediately north of the road.

The four walks are interconnected and, if desired, can be combined into one full-day. A single route or two are recommended. Please negotiate gates and stiles with care, keep strictly to the footpath or roadside, dress warmly and be prepared for wet conditions underfoot. Wear stout, waterproof shoes or boots and don't approach mine entrances, old shafts or ponds too closely. It is always better to walk with a companion. Before you depart, you may like to consult the interpretation board in the car park.

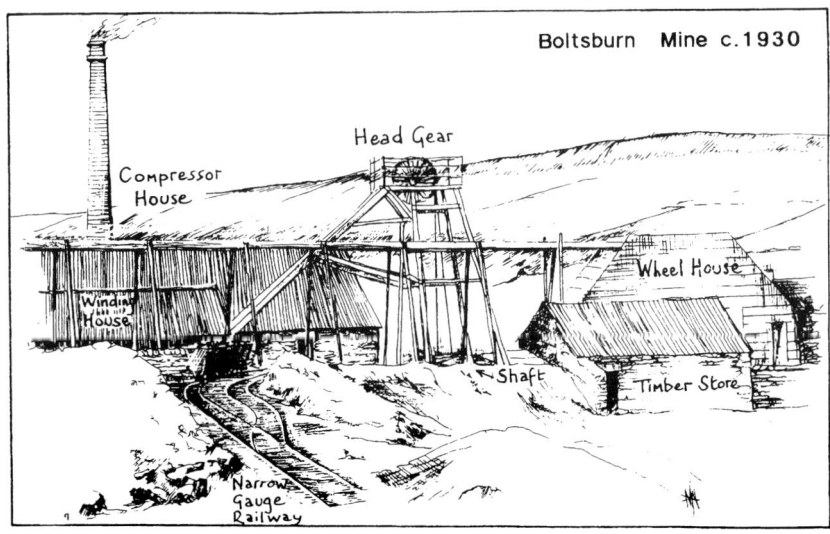

Boltsburn mine, washing-plant and Rookhope village.

The STARTING-POINT is the park next to the village hall in Boltsburn. Behind the hall is the school football field which once contained children's swings, a bowling green, tennis court and attractive wooden pavilion. This area was maintained by the Weardale Lead Company and funded by miners' subscriptions. Only the tennis court remains.

Summary: A walk highlighting the techniques and problems of mining and ore-dressing at Boltsburn, the vital role of railways and the chief elements of the village. Everywhere, there are marvellous views of the farmscape and the distant fell.

Before you leave the park, notice *a hole and debris (1)* in the private field over the fence. This was the first entrance into Boltsburn mine. It is situated just behind the line of buildings to the right. In more detail, the 'hole' was a short horizontal tunnel or level which then spiralled gradually underground allowing horses and men to descend easily into the mine.

WALK TO THE MAIN ROAD AND TURN RIGHT. On your left is the attractive, *grey granite war memorial* and to the right, the rear of a large, imposing *private house (2)*. This was the Weardale Lead Co's manager's residence, built c.1915. At first, the manager living here controlled the Rookhope mines only, but after 1947, all mining responsibility and administration in Weardale was transferred to Rookhope from Ireshopeburn. The house reflected the prestige attached to the job and the wealth of the Company. It was sold in 1980.

TURN RIGHT IMMEDIATELY PAST THE MANAGER'S HOUSE. Follow the unmetalled road between the house and Bolts Burn. The stream flows under Bolts Burn bridge eventually to join Rookhope Burn. On your left, across the burn, see *the Barrington Hall (3)* with its unusually high windows. Next to it is a stone house with a garden in front. This little complex once belonged to the Anglican church and was built with money given by Bishop Barrington of Durham in the early nineteenth century. The hall was used as a Sunday School and for village social gatherings. The cottage was occupied by the caretaker. Now the two buildings are joined as a private residence.

Before you leave, and this is not a leg-pull, imagine a standard-gauge railway squeezed into the narrow strip between the garden and Bolts Burn. From your right, the remarkable Bolts Law railway passed under the bridge and up the narrow valley as part of an amazing rail network centred on the village. We shall see and refer to this line more than once as the walk proceeds.

FOLLOW THE ROUGH ROAD TOWARDS THE FOOT/ROAD BRIDGE ACROSS ROOKHOPE BURN. Stop at the derelict buildings in front of the large house and gardens. Here were *the offices of the Lead Company* and at the end of the row, protruding at a right angle, is the old compressor house, once providing compressed air for underground drilling in Boltsburn mine.

CROSS THE RIVER AND PROCEED UP THE GENTLE SLOPE TOWARDS THE

LARGE GARAGES. The footbridge was much used by miners going to work at the second and main entrance to Boltsburn mine. Another crossing-point here was the old ford immediately downstream of the roadbridge.

Once across the footbridge, you encounter on the right *the grassed-over heaps of spoil* from the mine. Walk past these and the fingerpost on your left. Move up the rough road between the *haulage contractor's garages (4)* and the fenced-off, boarded-over *Boltsburn mine shaft (5)* to your right. DO NOT ATTEMPT TO STAND ON THE SHAFT! Some explanation of what happened here is necessary.

More lead ore came out of this shaft than from any other Weardale mine, except that at Burtree Pasture, near Cowshill. The shaft was sunk some 179 feet on to Boltsburn vein which ran across the main valley and slightly to the right (east) of Bolts Burn to beyond the horizon. The exact date of this venture is unknown but was probably begun by the Beaumonts c.1860. The shaft was widened during the mid-1880s when the infant Weardale Lead Company had ambitious plans. With the help of a new winding-engine, better pumps and a more powerful water-wheel, a larger entrance would allow better haulage of ore and more efficient drainage of the mine. Workings could now be extended more deeply and further away from the shaft.

The old horse level entry across the river could still be used by men and horses. Obviously, the level at the foot of the new shaft passed under the Rookhope Burn and joined with the existing level at the bottom of the spiral. In fact, the level from the shaft bottom eventually extended two miles and from it four underground shafts were sunk at successively lower levels to extract rich and large quantities of mineral favourably laid out in horizontal 'flats' under the hill in the distance.

So, near the point where you stand, there was,

(i) an enlarged winding-house with a steam-driven engine turning a drum and raising lead ore and 'deads' (waste) to the surface in large tubs from the shaft bottom or lowering timber etc. to the miners - much more efficient than the previous pulley system.

(ii) a water-wheel, in wooden casing to protect against the weather, which drove the rod pump (still remaining in the shaft), removing water from the mine.

(iii) a large compressor house (replacing the out-dated one near the old mine) which had a tall, square chimney and a system of 4" pipes feeding air under pressure across the river and into the old horse level to power rock drills and improve ventilation.

The accompanying drawing (page 6) gives an impression of the lay-out at Boltsburn mine in its prime. Closure finally came in 1931. The mine had been famous, successful and had put Rookhope on the map.

RETURN TOWARDS THE RIVER BUT AFTER A FEW YARDS, TURN LEFT ALONG THE FAIRLY WIDE TRACK OPPOSITE THE GARAGES. You will see a blocked entrance to the left and in line with the shaft. This was an *inspection tunnel,* allowing maintenance of the pumps inside the shaft.

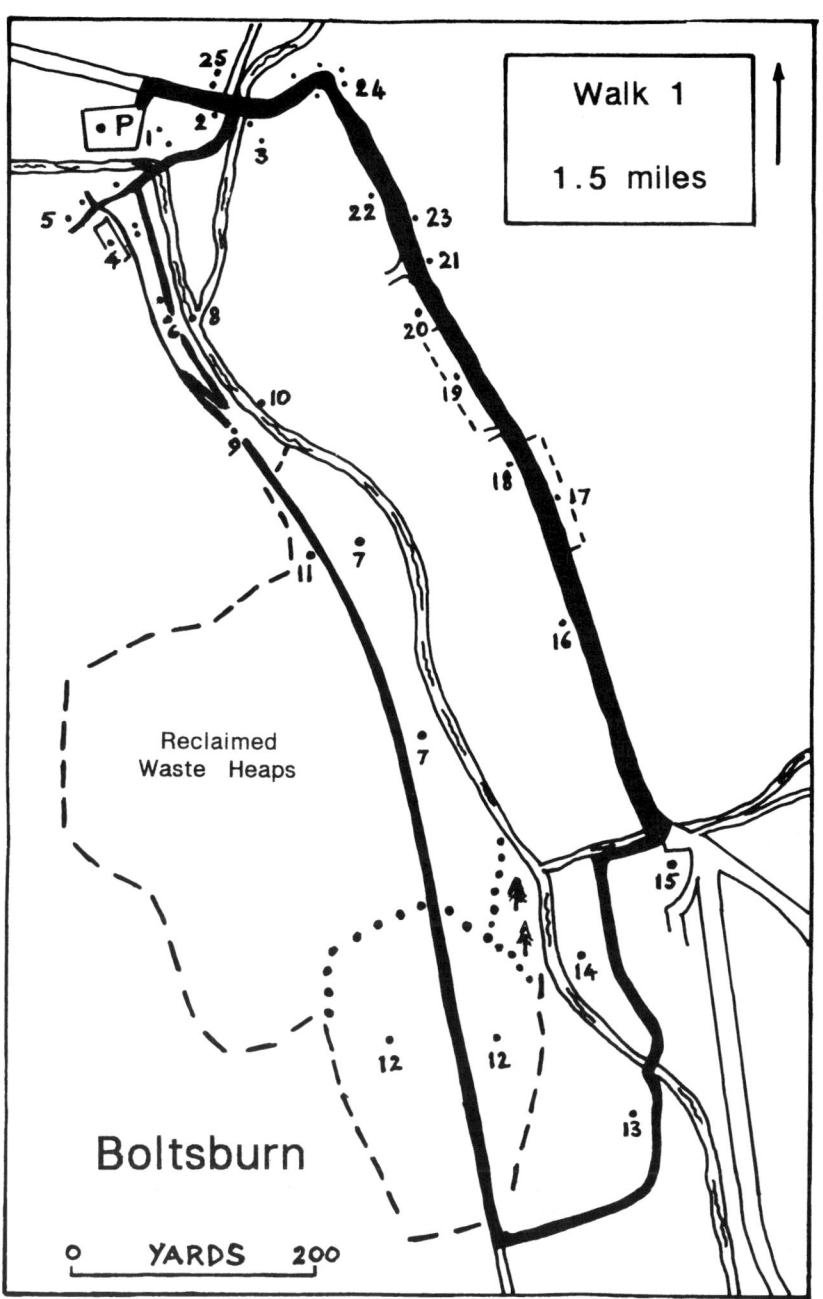

Walk 1

1.5 miles

Reclaimed
Waste Heaps

Boltsburn

0   YARDS   200

9

RETURN TOWARDS THE RIVER. TURN RIGHT AT THE FINGERPOST AND FOLLOW THE TRACK ALONGSIDE THE RIVER. THE TRACK MAY BE WET IN PLACES. The heavily mineralised, orange-coloured running water and general wetness stem from a blocked-up *underground drainage level* to your right. The very top of the arched exit might be partially visible at track level on the right. The arch connected with the top of the Boltsburn shaft about 100 yards away. It had two functions:

(i) deads from the mine could be trammed by horse or locomotive to be deposited on spoil heaps across the river (see below).

(ii) water pumped up the mine shaft was discharged along it into the river.

For safety reasons, the arched entrance was closed in the 1950s which led to poor surface drainage and waterlogging. The problem has been compounded by the collapse and disappearance of another, *earlier drainage level* (from the same mine) which was just a few yards further downstream from the arch - close to two unrelated, modern drainage pipes. A careful glance into the river bank will reveal a square-shaped outlet which was part of this system.

As you walk, the remains of *stone structures (6)* mark part of the first washing-floor of Boltsburn mine. Ore or bouse was carried from the shaft on a narrow-gauge track (along the top road above your viewpoint) and tipped into bays or bousesteads - their remnants can still be seen.

Before this, however, the lead ore from the earlier horse level had been trammed over the river and along the track to the bays where you stand. The tramway bridge, close to the footbridge, has long since gone.

A blacksmith's shop and workshop also stood near the storage bays. As you can see, the line of the tramway then continued further to Boltsburn Washing, *a later dressing-floor (7)* where the mix of rock and ore was washed, broken up and separated. All the physical evidence has disappeared - but see below.

Very near the old bays are two other points of interest. First, notice on the side of your route, *a small concrete pillar* with a metal cap. This is the point where Professor K. C. Dunham, Durham University, former Director of the Geological Survey, chose to drill into the local rocks to investigate the probability of a granite dome at some depth. This dome, he thought, might explain the rich mineralisation of the North Pennines. At a depth of c.1,400', grey granite was found. (See also Walk 2)

Secondly, *the stone pier (8)* standing on the paved river bed marks the point where the standard-gauge Boltslaw railway crossed Rookhope Burn to join with *the Rookhope Middlehope line (9)*, the track of which is immediately above you.

WALK BEYOND THE BAYS AND THEN RIGHT, AFTER ABOUT 100 YARDS; UP THE ERODED RAMP ON TO THE TOP TRACK. Look across the river and appreciate how wooden trestles were needed to carry the Boltslaw railway as it approached this junction. The river-stone pier has crumbled badly recently and may soon be lost.

Rookhope from the south. Stotfield Burn (foreground) and Boltsburn (centre) mark the beginning of the village. Expansion of the two has resulted in a winding, linear settlement.

Boltsburn mine (walks 1, 2, 3). The disused mine shaft occupies the centre of the scene. Behind are the village primary school, the village hall and a few houses. The crumbling mine smithy is on the right.

Stotfield Burn (walk 1). The C13 farm and the later dwellings straddle the tributary stream. The desolate ruins of the fluorspar mine lie further up-valley. On the open fell is Wright's ironstone quarry. Overlooking "Stots" is St. John's church. In the foreground are the sludge pits of Boltsburn Washing.

Lintzgarth Smelt-mill site (walk 2). The stone arch is the solitary survivor of the mill buildings. A double flue conducted gases from the furnaces above a series of six arches to the gently sloping moorland flue. Two small arched remnants of this flue have been preserved.

For the next half mile, keep to the old Rookhope-Middlehope railway line. It gives you level walking except for the potholes and pools. Take care. The views of the valley, farmland, village and river are wonderful.

Spot *the low, grassed-over spoil heaps (10)*, mentioned above, and now eroded by the river. The north abutments of the disappeared bridge at the end of the heaps are still there. Recall that this debris came from the two Boltsburn mines – but see also West Level on Walk 2.

Some explanation of the railway line where you walk is necessary. It came to Rookhope in 1854 and was laid by the Weardale Iron Company, not the Weardale Lead Company, which did, however, benefit from it. The railway initially ran from Middlehope, near Westgate, to Boltsburn, a distance of 4 miles, where it linked with the Boltslaw line. *The garages (4)* have replaced the old railway sheds.

Originally, its main purpose was to move iron ore and limestone from Middlehope via Boltsburn up the steep hill side to Bolts Law and then to Tow Law where the Iron Company had its blast furnaces and foundry. In due course, during the early 1860s, more ironworking in the Rookhope Burn valley, west of Boltsburn, extended the railway and also added pigs (bars) of lead from the Lintzgarth smelt-mill to the freight it carried out of Weardale (Walk 2). Coal for Rookhope and Westgate was a vital return commodity.

The Middlehope line ran through another of Rookhope's great contributions to the North Pennines' lead-mining industry. Unfortunately, almost all of its visible remains have been destroyed. *The Boltsburn washing-plant (7)* in its size and complexity was remarkable – and unique. Extending from river level and far up the valley slope to your right, the complex was started by the Weardale Lead Co. in 1903 to process the galena (lead ore) from Boltsburn mine but, over the years, minerals from other mines were also fed in. This new development completely replaced the antiquated dressing-plant, noted above.

From time to time, as circumstances changed, modifications were introduced at the plant. In brief, lead ore at Boltsburn Washing was fed in at one end and lead concentrate, ready for transport and smelting, emerged at the other. These most intricate of activities were performed day and night and required a system of railways, inclines, aerial flights, hoppers, dams, races, waterwheels, supplies of coal, oil, electricity (after 1937), timber and the provision of large buildings containing crushing rollers, jiggers and separating tables. Additionally, space was found for settling troughs, sludge pits – the latter have actually survived – as well as the great heaps of waste. All these were crowded into the area shown on your map. Processing finally stopped in the late 1970s and demolition followed soon afterwards.

Perhaps a drawing (page 15) is the best way to appreciate the industrial scene at its peak in the 1920s. The main elements were:

(i) the Middlehope railway (J) which ran at a higher level than the buildings next to the river (see the key to the sketch) It pre-dated everything else. However, after the opening of the new plant, mines in the highest part of the Rookhope valley began to use this line as far

13

as Boltsburn mine. A short ramp then transferred their ore to trucks on a narrow-gauge line (K) going to the washing-plant from Boltsburn and West Level (Walk 2).

(ii) the enclosed water-wheel (E), powering the crushing and jigging machinery (D, C), was fed by water race (I) and a piped supply from the two dams (P, O).

(iii) incoming ore from Boltsburn mine, West Level (Walk 2) and others was carried along the narrow-gauge railway (K) and tipped into a hopper (L) under the gantry.

(iv) dressed ore or concentrate was hauled in trucks half way up an incline (M), then to the railway (N) which connected with (K) and thence continuously to the Lintzgarth smelter, one mile away. Trucks, disposing of waste from the dressing area, also used the incline. As the mountain of waste (Q) increased, an aerial flight (R) was introduced to lift it to higher levels.

KEY TO DRAWING

A Table House where fine particles of galena were separated from waste with water flowing across an inclined table.

B The foreman's cabin.

C The jigger-house where crushed ore and stone were shaken in water troughs allowing the denser ore to sink to the bottom.

D The crushing-house where metal rollers were turned to break down larger pieces of stone and ore.

E The wheel-house with a rotating water-wheel driving the crusher and the jiggers.

F The auxiliary engine house using oil fuel should the water supply prove inadequate.

G Oil-storage shed.

H Blacksmith's shop used to repair and replace machinery.

I A long water race carrying water from Rookhope Burn to the wheel-house.

J The Rookhope-Middlehope railway line.

K The narrow-gauge mineral line to the Lintzgarth smelter via Boltsburn mine.

L The hopper at the end of the above line where crude ore was stored.

M Railway incline which raised dressed lead to the outgoing railway and spoil to the waste heaps.

N The return railway to the smelt-mill; joining with (K).

O Storage dam giving a head of water for the wheel and other processes.

P Holding dam, feeding the lower storage dam.

Q Waste heaps with a high fluorspar content.

R Aerial flight to ease the problem of waste disposal.

Boltsburn   Washing c.1920

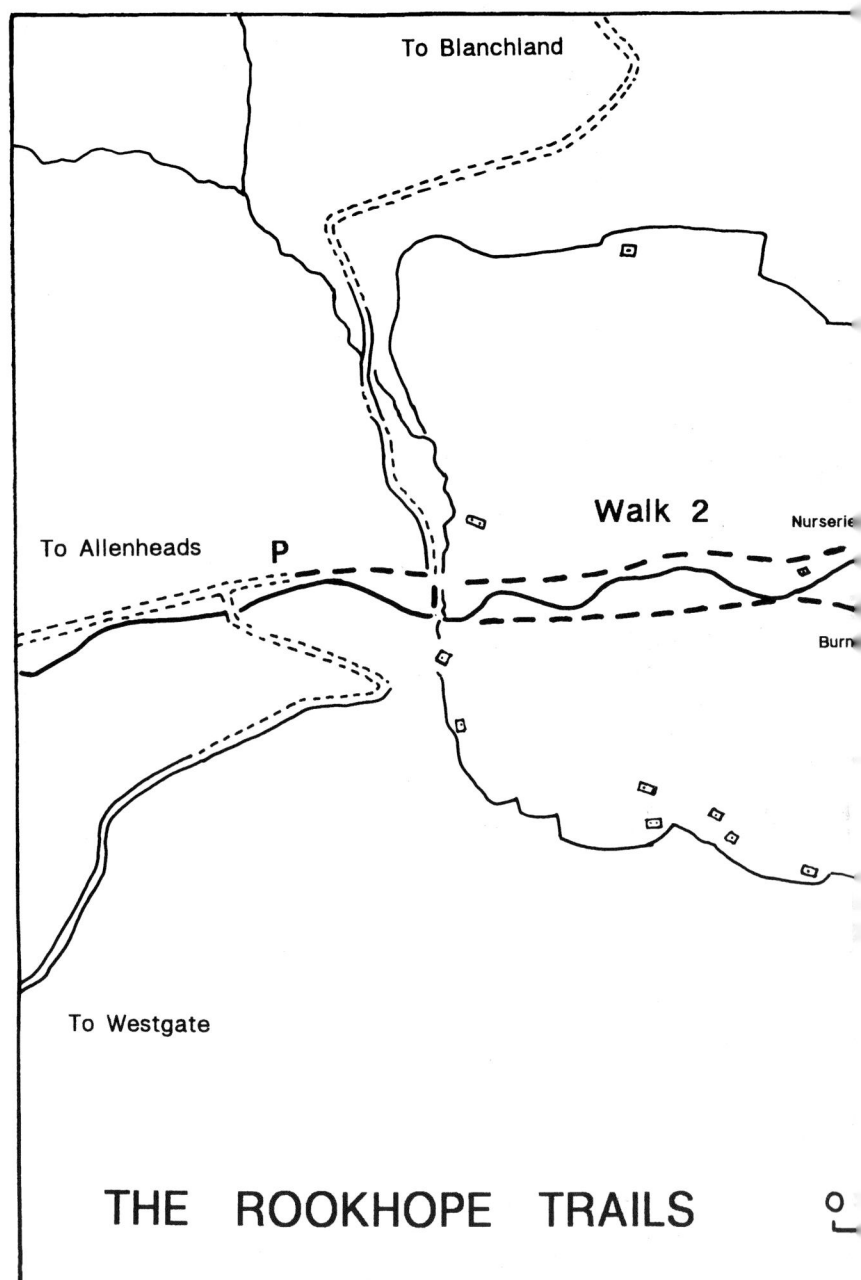

To Blanchland

To Allenheads   **P**   **Walk 2**   Nurserie

Burn

To Westgate

THE ROOKHOPE TRAILS

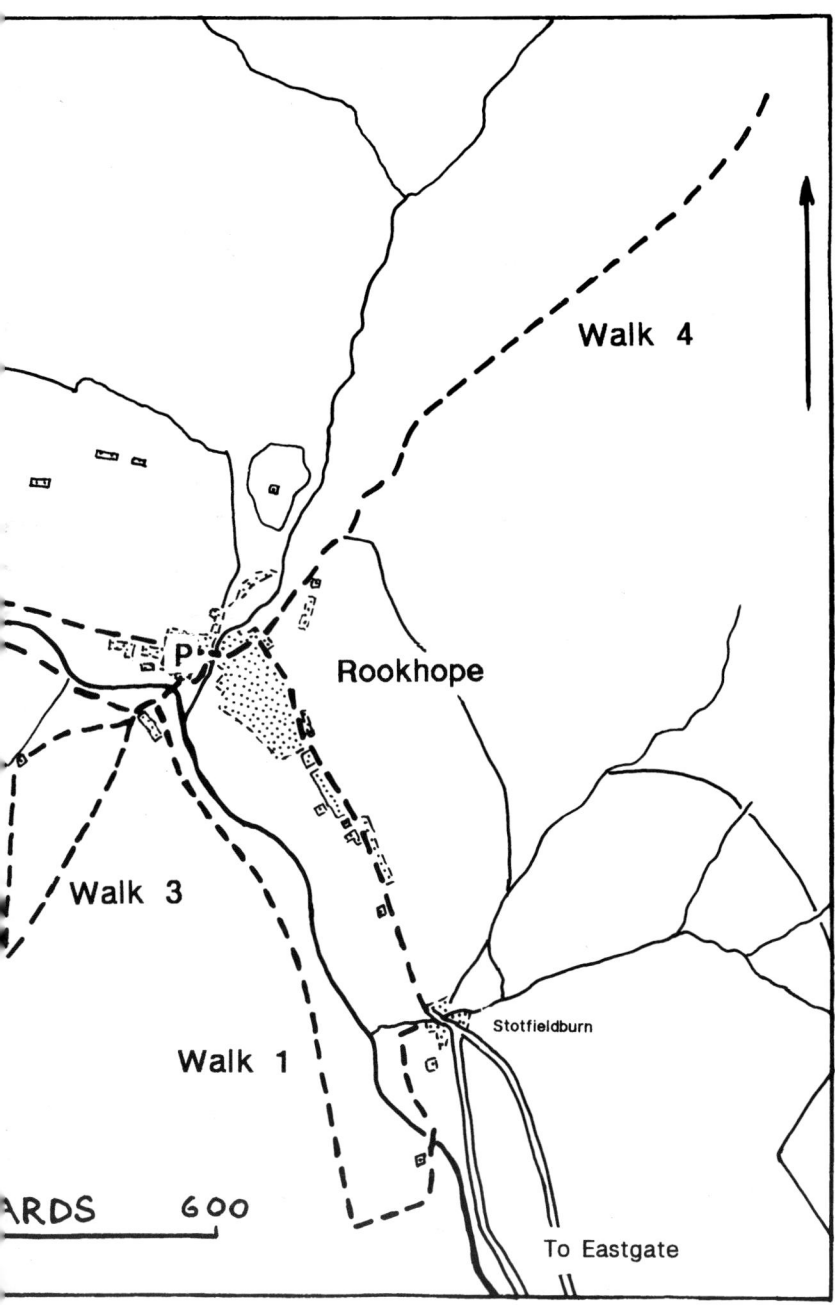

Walk 4

Rookhope

Walk 3

Walk 1

Stotfieldburn

To Eastgate

RDS   600

When the Lintzgarth smelt-mill closed (1919) and the Bolts Law railway ceased (1923), Boltsburn Washing had to find both a new smelter and a new transport route. Yet more ingenuity resulted in a 3-mile aerial flight to the main Weardale railway line near Eastgate. Thus, galena to Tyneside for smelting and increasing amounts of fluorspar to Teesside were carried out while coal came by return. The system ended in 1947 when lorry transport took over.

Back to the walk along the railway line. Near the northern entrance to the former washing area are some *old concrete supports (11)* on the slope to your right. These stand in front of the lower, partially filled-in dam which is out of your vision and off the footpath. THE DAM SHOULD NOT BE VISITED. Issuing freely on to the bottom road is water from an underground pipe which continues to drain the dam. The concrete pillars are the remains of hoppers where coal brought in by the aerial flight was stored next to the narrow-gauge railway.

At the exit of the plant, *sludge beds (12)* lie to your left. Those to the right were lost during the rather crude landscaping which followed the commercial excavation of the huge waste heaps, rich in fluorspar, during the early 1980s. The sludge pits were dumps for useless material pumped from the washing-floor. Some of the waste was also spread further up the slope. The generally desolate, wet, eroded appearance marks the failure to use the correct grass seed on the poor soil. Where good seed was used, slightly to the north, the green cover is a better outcome.

From your viewpoint, look across the valley to the Stotfield Burn tributary. The tiny huddle of buildings, St. John's Anglican church and a few mining ruins up the valley define the eastern end of the village. Fell House on the curving head dyke from Stotfield to Boltsburn, between the pasture land and the open fell, can be clearly seen. Incidentally, a stot was a young beast.

Stotfield was the second of Rookhope's great mines. However, it was never operated by the Blackett-Beaumonts. Before the Weardale Lead Co. obtained the lease, a number of small private firms were involved here and at Thorney Brow and Brandon Walls further down valley - unusually, the lessor of all three was the Durham Dean and Chapter and not the Bishop.

Although the 'Stots' remains are not along your walk, it's worth noting that after 1900, the mine produced large amounts of fluorspar, dressed at Boltsburn Washing, but closure came in 1966 more than 30 years after Boltsburn. This had a severe effect on village employment as well as the viability of the dressing-plant.

CONTINUE WALKING. THERE ARE TWO GATES. TURN LEFT AT THE SECOND, THEN OVER A STILE AND WIND YOUR WAY CAREFULLY DOWN THE SLOPE. *Empty Waterside farm buildings (13)* are ahead on the valley bottom. GO THOUGH THE GATE TO THE RIGHT OF THE FARM, across the river and through a kissing-gate. Follow Church Lonnen with two cemeteries on your left and right. *The older (14)* was the site of Rookhope's earlier Anglican church - Holy Trinity built in 1840 - and demolished because of wet foundations in favour of St. John's. Behind the high wall on the right are the gardens and former vicarage of both churches.

TURN RIGHT ALONG THE LANE TO STOTFIELD BURN. The stream is on your left as you enter a *small cluster of four or five houses (15).* At the heart of the white dwellings was a public house, convenient for Stots' miners. Notice the empty farm premises over the bridge which are now storage buildings. This was the location of the C13 cattle shieling which is, by far, the oldest occupied site in the cluster.

TURN LEFT AT STOTS. FOLLOW THE ROAD INTO THE VILLAGE. Another *disused farm (16),* now a private house, looms on the left. The village's unique football field lay on the land between the old farm and the river - unique because it was on two levels and pretty bumpy everywhere! Now climb gently to Chapel Row and the footpath on your right. Originally, Chapel Row was isolated mid-way between Stots and Boltsburn. It grew in the early C19 and included *the Primitive Methodist chapel (17)* of 1836, once located in the vacant space in the terrace. The chapel fell into disuse in 1863 to make way for *a larger building (18)* on the other side of the road. Both the second chapel and a shop next to it have since been converted to houses.

NOW WALK THROUGH THE CENTRE OF THE VILLAGE. 1929 *Hogarth Terrace (19)* to the left, reflects previous mining prosperity. Pass the *large detached house (20),* the former Co-op store (c.1907), *the old workmens Club (21)* first right and, on the left, a succession of houses, former shops and *the 1863 Wesleyan Methodist chapel (22)* - the village's first chapel (1812) lay almost opposite the present one at *the first small cottage (23),* just a few yards down the road.

Arrive at *the Post Office,* the last retail survivor. Directly opposite, across the main road, is another converted farm. Before the farm, however, *the 1819 Barrington school (24)* stood here and next to it, on the left as you view from the Post Office, was *the village smithy.*

PROCEED DOWN THE STEEP BEND. Immediately on your right is an empty foundation on which *the Miners' Institute* - a male preserve - provided a reading room and meeting place. Continue to the tumbledown, derelict farm and cobbled farm-yard (right) which ceased long ago to be *the village corn mill.*

Now pass Rookhope Inn and note its *small storage building* beside the bridge. It is probable that the *stone houses (25)* behind the war memorial were the location of Boltsburn's first farm, another C13 shieling similar to that at Stotfield Burn. The walk now ends at the village hall.

WALK 2:

Lintzgarth Smelt Mill

Summary: An easy, valley-bottom walk, west of Rookhope, past three defunct mines and a lodging-shop; along two railway tracks and a water race to the site of an C18 smelt mill. You are close to Rookhope Burn throughout. Roadside return via Rookhope Nurseries and the Victorian Board school.

Begin at the village hall car park. To avoid duplication of information, follow Walk 1 as far as *Boltsburn shaft (5)* which is marked as (1) on your Lintzgarth route map (p.23).

TURN RIGHT (WEST) AT THE FINGERPOST NEAR THE MINE SHAFT. You are now walking along the narrow-gauge tramway which connected *Boltsburn shaft (1)* and *West Level mine (2)* to the 1903 Boltsburn Washing, a quarter of a mile to the south (see walk 1). Continue to the wet entrance of West Level. Here you see the problem of underground water in mines and the deterioration in the arched level since closure in 1942.

The Weardale Iron Co. opened this mine in the late 1850s and originally laid the railway track from the entrance to the junction with the Company's Bolts Law and Middlehope lines (Walk 1). When the iron deposits supplying Tow Law were worked out, the Weardale Lead Co. took over and the railway was rerouted and extended. Just south of Boltsburn mine, it joined with a new, slightly higher line running between Boltsburn Washing (Walk 1) and Lintzgarth smelt mill. A stretch of this 1'10" narrow gauge track can still be seen between the fence and the wall, just above West Level entrance.

From the mine portal, look across the river to the *1872 Board school (3)*, its sports field and the *tennis court (4)*. Left to right, the four defunct farms above the school are Rimey Law, High House, Lovely Hall and High House.

FROM WEST LEVEL, WALK THE SHORT DISTANCE TO THE WALL AND THEN DOWN THE SLOPE TO THE GRASS TRACK AND STILE. High to your left, *three stone piers (6)* once carried a race bringing water to the water wheels at Boltsburn mine and the washing-plant. You are now walking along the Iron Company standard-gauge track (5) extended up-valley from the Bolts Law-Middlehope junction in the 1860s.

An *old weir* built across Rookhope Burn formerly diverted water to the early Boltsburn washing-floor before the 1903 reorganisation. The weir and the race have been completely eroded. Continue along the railway until it disappears as a result of severe flooding in January 1995. CLIMB LEFT ON TO THE NARROW-GAUGE TRACK. THIS IS THE LINE RUNNING BETWEEN BOLTSBURN WASHING AND LINTZGARTH MILL. *Foulwood Mine (7)* is straight ahead. It was primarily an ironstone mine and ceased working in the later C19.

Follow the railway. There are *more water race pillars (9)* to the left and *an early C.20 miners' lodging-shop (8)* on the right. This large two-storey building provided week-day accommodation for those whose homes were distant. It is a clear indication that labour was

Foulwood (Burnside) shops (walk 2). This rather austere, early C20 building, providing accommodation for miners, was one of many scattered throughout the North Pennines.

Peg's Hole reservoir (walk 3). The dam was built in 1904 on Smailsburn Common to feed water under gravity to Boltsburn Washing. The embankment is still in perfect condition. In the distance, the earlier farm buildings of Rimey Law, High House and Lovely Hall can be seen just below the sharp line separating the inby (improved) land from the outby heather fell.

Bolts Law railway summit, 1670' above sea level (walk 4). These buildings are all that remains after 70 years' decay and demolition. The engine house for the locomotives, taking wagons to or from the Bolts Law incline, is on the right. Next to it are the base of the chimney and the winding-house, containing a standing-engine and the winding-drums. The railway tracks are right of the buildings.

Rookhope village from Broaddale (walk 3). The school (left), the mines' manager's house (centre) and newer estate of Boltsburn Crescent (right) can be seen. Also visible are the Bolts Law railway and, to its right, Hylton Terrace and Fell House.

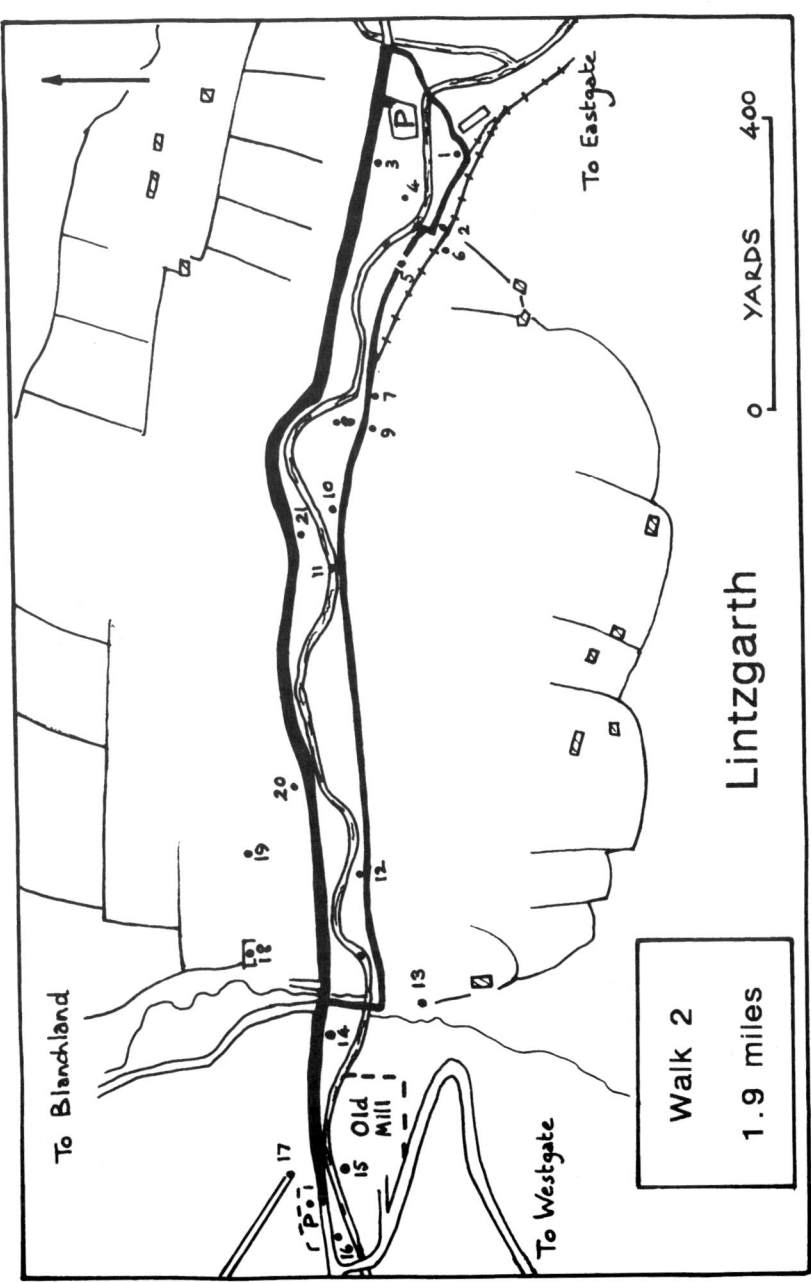

To Eastgate

YARDS

400

0

Lintzgarth

To Blandland

Old Mill

To Westgate

Walk 2
1.9 miles

23

in short supply. It now houses lengths of the granite core extracted during the 1961 borehole experiment (walk 1). The short brick terrace of Burnside behind the 'shops' was added c.1925, another sign of mining prosperity.

CLIMB THE STILE AND CONTINUE ALONG THE TRACK. Both railways now run closely together for some distance. *Rookhope Nurseries (10)* is a complex of modern greenhouses, caravans and a house *Brook Cottage (21)* across the river. CROSS THE STILE. Just beyond the Nurseries, the Iron Co. railway veers right while the Lead Co. narrow-gauge line goes straight on. *A railway bridge (11)*, no longer visible, carried the standard-gauge line to the north side of the river and up to the smelt-mill.

Your walk is now well-defined along the narrow track - note the use of mine debris in the embankment. Notice, too, *the Boltsburn race* on the left and, after the gate, the point where it passed *under the railway (12)*. The *control weir* has been washed away. Left of the stile, *the white Lintzgarth C13 shieling (13)* has seen better days as efforts are now made to rescue it. As you cross the stile, a *large stone arch (15)* lies in front of you and *two smaller arches (17)* above the main road to the right. You are now looking across the largely empty site of the Lintzgarth smeltmill.

CROSS THE STILE AND TURN RIGHT OFF THE RAILWAY. DESCEND TO THE FOOTBRIDGE ACROSS ROOKHOPE BURN. To the left before you cross, is wet, neglected land where a race, having supplied the smelt-mill, re-entered the river.

The tramway you have walked along came to an end at *Rookhope (Lintzgarth) smelt mill (15)* which occupied the level ground between the river and the road rising south towards Westgate. The forlorn, solitary arch is the most conspicuous relic of a set of buildings whose purpose was to smelt lead concentrate from the Boltsburn dressing-floor (and others further up-valley) into pigs of lead and also to refine small quantities of silver from the molten lead.

The mill was constructed during the 1730s by the mines' lessee, Sir Walter Blackett. It replaced a C17 smelter on the same bank, a quarter of a mile upstream, all trace of which has gone. The Lintzgarth mill worked until 1919. During almost 200 years, several changes in design and lay-out were necessary.

The first version probably had a vertical chimney on the mill site to dispose of the sulphurous fumes. Peat rather than coal was burned. At some stage, two horizontal stone flues, supported by six arches, were introduced. They carried the poisonous gases across the river and the road and then into a gently inclined chimney extending up the valley side to a vertical stack. The latter no longer exists but the line of the deroofed double flue is unmistakable as you approach the mill site. The total length of the chimney across Redburn Common is $1\frac{1}{2}$. miles. It is likely that the flues were extended up the slope in two stages. As pointed out above, a small fragment of the dual arching in the flue can be seen on the north side of the road. THERE IS NO PUBLIC ACCESS.

There were doorways into the flues and condensing chambers - wider portions at the side of the chimney where the swirling gases were encouraged to condense and deposit their lead. At intervals, water was washed down the chimney and the lead collected in small ponds. One such collecting point, known as a *fume tank,* was situated on the site of the roadside car park.

TURN LEFT AT THE STILE LEADING ON TO THE MAIN ROAD, JUST WEST OF THE CATTLE GRID. As you approach the stile, a storm gate across Red Burn can be seen - this prevented animals from straying too far, either voluntarily or in flood water.

When the iron trade fell away, the Lead Company made great use of the standard-gauge railway passing next to the mill:

(i) its proximity to the mill and the bigger trucks it conveyed led to the disuse of the narrow-gauge line across the river. Perhaps the two systems overlapped for some time. It was much more efficient, however, to bring dressed lead from Boltsburn Washing (and others further up-valley) by standard gauge to *a siding alongside the road (16),* tram it across the river into the storage bays at the mill, have it smelted and the lead carried out as return freight.

(ii) *a second siding (14)* was therefore necessary, with a connecting ramp (still visible) down to the river and a bridge (not visible) across to the mill. This allowed the rapid loading of lead pigs and direct transport to the Bolts Law incline.

Transport in and out of the mill was not the only problem. Large quantities of water were also required, not least to drive a water-wheel powering the bellows to raise the smelting temperatures. From the car park, it is possible to look across the Westgate road and pick out the main incoming feeder race.

Eventually, old age, newer smelting methods and the option of transporting the lead concentrate by aerial flight (to the railway at Eastgate) or lorry overtook the mill which was forced to close. It slowly fell into ruin and in the 1950s all but one of the splendid arches were pulled down for building stone. The remaining arch is a listed building. THERE IS NO PUBLIC ACCESS.

RETURN TO THE BOLTSBURN CAR PARK ALONG THE MAIN ROAD. WALK CAREFULLY. *Redburn farm (18),* another C13 foundation, is still active. *Redburn mine (19)* - worked by ICI between 1963-80 for fluorspar - is shrouded by *recent conifers (20)* occupying the former cricket field! *Rookhope Nurseries, Foulwood shops and the primary school* are passed again en route as you arrive at the car park beside the village hall.

Peg's Hole Dam via Boltsburn Mine

Summary: A fairly vigorous walk up and down moderate gradients across rough fell land. Mining relics include an early C 20 power dam, water races and narrow-gauge railway track. There are glorious views of Rookhope village and surrounding landscape.

Beginning at Boltsburn car park, follow the route described in Walk 1 as far as *Boltsburn mine (5)*. You are now at (1) on the Peg's Hole map. From this point, walking is uphill across open fell. Stout, waterproof footwear is recommended. Leave the mine shaft and CROSS THE STILE behind *the contractor's garage. The disused blacksmith's shop* and the concrete pillars of an oil tank, once used by the compressor house at the mine, are to the left. At the foot of the stile, note the *narrow track of the old railway* laid between Boltsburn Washing and Lintzgarth smelt-mill. IMMEDIATELY BEYOND THE STILE, TURN HALF RIGHT AND FOLLOW THE FOOTPATH.

About 35 yards from the stile, you cross *the water race* described in Walk 2 which supplied water along a wooden launder to the wheel at Boltsburn mine - the race is best seen 10 yards to the right of the path where some of its paving has collapsed. It also continued, more indistinctly, to the left (south) of the path to a dam at Boltsburn Washing.

A fenced shaft (left) can be clearly seen near the race. This and other shafts on the walk are very much earlier than Boltsburn mine, C17 at least. They indicate a centuries-old knowledge of the Boltsburn vein. Such shafts were primitive. They were sunk several feet until the problem of vertical haulage, water, bad air and the risk of collapse made work impossible. Usually, a line of surface shafts following the vein can be traced.

Another small man-made feature is *a square brick-lined hole (2),* beside a grassed shaft, a few yards further on, to the right. Up to the mine closure, water was stored and fed from here under gravity to the compressor house and the winding-engine boilers next to the Boltsburn shaft. Follow the path upwards across rush and grass vegetation to *Broad Dale House (3)* on the edge of the fell. The deserted house and earth closets have been abandoned to farm animals and nature, another sign of population contraction into the village.

Admire the magnificent views to the north including:

(i) the winding track of the Bolts Law railway (Walk 4)

(ii) the old sandstone (for house-building) and ironstone quarries spread along the fell to the right of the railway

(iii) the school, the Boltsburn cluster of houses and the linear growth to the east.

CLIMB HIGHER FROM BROAD DALE, FOLLOWING THE STRAIGHT WALL ON YOUR RIGHT. The path has been lost among thick rushes. After some 300 yards, the wall changes direction. CONTINUE ALONG IT for c.100 yards and arrive at *Peg's Hole reservoir (1,300')* surrounded by a barbed wire fence (5). DO NOT CROSS THIS FENCE.

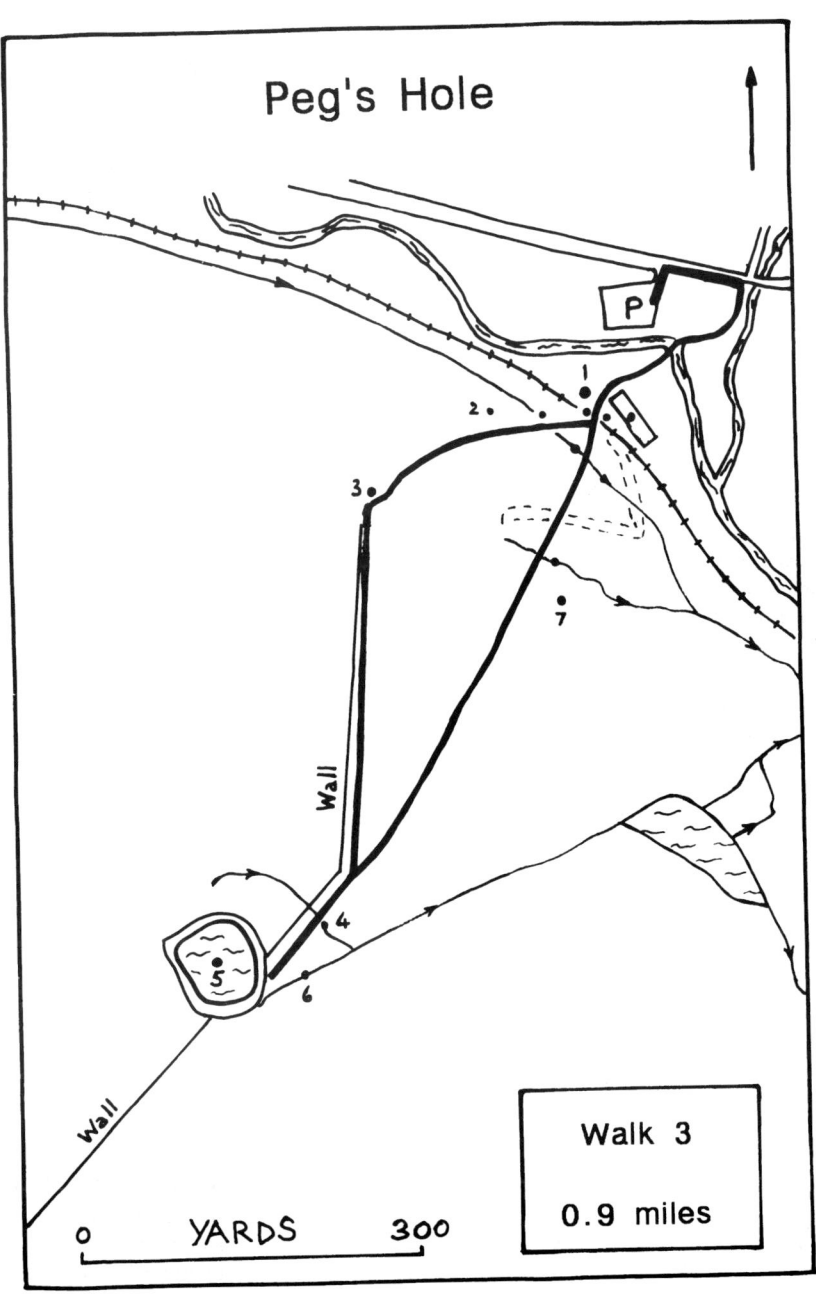

Peg's Hole

P

1
2
3
Wall
4
5
6
7

0 YARDS 300

Walk 3

0.9 miles

The lead industry required considerable, guaranteed quantities of water. Sometimes, during summer, even the Rookhope valley was affected by drought. Big gravity-feed reservoirs were therefore essential for large-scale operations. The Weardale Lead Company constructed Peg's Hole in 1904 to supply its new Boltsburn dressing-plant. Typically, the site of the dam is on a gentle slope which gave a natural back wall while earth dug out from the reservoir base was piled up into a semi-circular embankment.

To ensure permanency of supply, another dam was also made a mile further west and linked to Peg's Hole. Initially, the water from Peg's Hole was led down the *open channel (6)*, now a water-filled ditch, to a dam next to the plant. Later, a more efficient underground piped supply was used.

RETURN AT FIRST ALONG THE SAME ROUTE. You will cross *a small feeder race (4)* passing under the wall and connecting with the large ditch. LEAVE THE WALL WHERE IT CHANGES DIRECTION AND CONTINUE IN A STRAIGHT LINE FOR 400 YARDS. There is no properly defined footpath and the fell terrain is rough and uneven. In the distance, the *remote magazine house (7)* which stored the dynamite and detonators for blasting rock in the mines, is easily seen. Use it as a marker but pass by about 30 yards to its left.

The valley panorama is superb. As you descend, there are more old shafts to right and left. *Two water races* cross your route, just before and after a modern earth track used by farm tractors. Both are shown on your map. The bottom race is a continuation of the one walked past at the beginning, near the stile. Both races join and enter the lower of the two dams at the washing-plant and are very much older than the Peg's Hole system. Before you return via the smithy to the stile and Boltsburn mine, notice the the line of the narrow-gauge railway, ahead and to the right of you, as it makes it way south to the site of the washing-plant. RETURN TO THE MAIN ROAD AND CAR PARK.

⟞⟝⟝•◦•⟞⟝

WALK 4:

Boltslaw

Summary: A steady climb of 600 feet for $1\frac{1}{4}$ miles to Bolts Law summit (1,670') along a mid-C.19 railway line, unique in the U. K. The walk can be shortened at any point and the return journey made to Rookhope. A walk stirring the imagination and providing peace, solitude and magnificent panoramas of the village and its valley. Good visibility is necessary.

Leave the Boltsburn car park and turn right to follow the main road to the *post office (1)*.

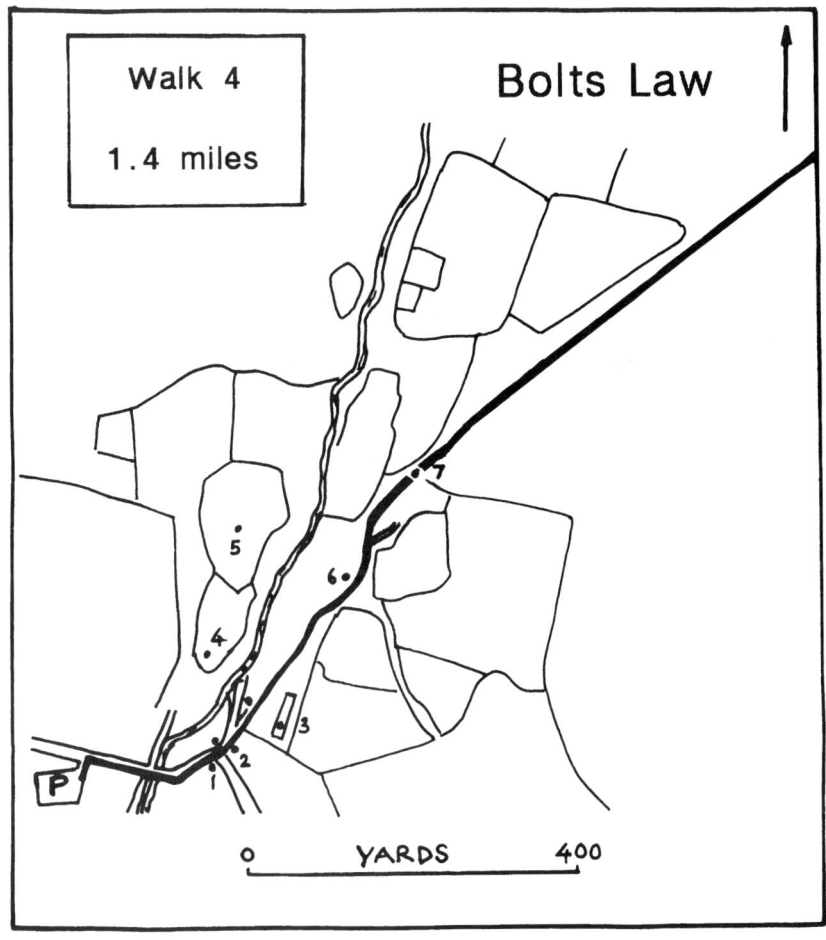

The grassed-over platform of the *former village institute* and the *Barrington school building (2)* (Walk 1) are on the opposite side of the road.

WALK UP THE ROUGH ROAD FROM THE POST-OFFICE WITH THE OLD SCHOOL AND DISUSED BLACKSMITH'S SHOP ON YOUR RIGHT. You will see a higher footpath to the right which winds up to mid-nineteenth century *Hylton Terrace (3),* now much renovated with extensions and properties joined together. The terrace is still known as Blue Row because it had the first Welsh slates in the village.

THE ROUGH ROAD QUICKLY DIVIDES. KEEP LEFT FOR A FEW YARDS. You will spot a *ruined weir with a waterfall* in the valley bottom. A race once ran from here to the derelict corn mill, next to the institute. Facing you across the river is an unusually large stone 'wall'. This structure was a pier for a high, wooden, trestle-type bridge which supported the Bolts Law standard-gauge line. The remarkable bridge has obviously been removed but cast your eye to the left of the wall and trace the long-overgrown, faint mark of the track which passed under the road-bridge near the car park.

Also across the river, the plight of Pennine farming is emphasised by yet another *farm desertion (4).* RETURN TO THE JUNCTION AND TURN SHARP LEFT UP THE ROUGH ROAD. Immediately on the left are the scanty foundations of an *aerial flight terminal* next to a building. At this point, ganister rock from a quarry further up the Bolts Burn valley was stored for removal by lorry.

Keep to the unmade road until a *sizeable, gated compound (6)* appears. Inside, an eye-catching notice, "Trespassers will be shot" reminds you not to enter! Instead, walk behind this collection of miscellanea and on to a narrow grass footpath. You have now arrived at the incredible Bolts Law, single track, upland railway stretching into the distance - in its prime, the compound was a coal-siding and depot for Rookhope. Railway wagons led coal along the top of the 'teems' and tipped it into the storage bays.

THE REST OF THIS UPHILL WALK IS ALONG THE RAILWAY. At the top of the long incline at Bolts Law about a mile from where you stand, a winding-house with a standing-engine controlled the movement of trucks by wire rope. Coal was needed to heat the boilers and drive the steam-powered engine. A tall chimney created a strong draught and a flue for the smoke and gases. There was also an engine shed for the locomotives involved in the next stage of the 4-mile journey to Park Head on the Stanhope and Tyne railway. A few cottages for railway workers also existed. These have disappeared but the circular base of the chimney and the shells of the winding-house and the engine sheds are still visable.

The purpose of this line, the highest-ever standard-gauge railway in the United Kingdom, was to haul iron ore and limestone from the Rookhope terminus to the Tow Law iron-works as well as pigs of lead to the Tyne. Coal was brought as return freight. The venture was completed in 1846 by Charles Attwood's Weardale Iron Company. It came to an end in 1923 shortly after run-away trucks fell from the trestle bridge. The height difference between Boltsburn and Bolts Law is 600' and the length of the line $1\frac{1}{4}$ miles, an average gradient of 1 in 11.

The gaunt Bolts Law remains lie off your map but there is no danger of you losing your way. Simply follow the line to the horizon to discover the ruined engine shed, drum house and the base of the chimney. As you progress up the incline, see another former farm (5) across the valley. The stile (7) marks the end of the enclosed farm land, thence it's open fell all the way.

You go through a number of cuttings and, at one point, watch for a wider path which contained the double track where the descending trucks passed those en route for Bolts Law. To your left, there are marvellous views of small C.18 fields and the C.13 shieling of Bolts Walls. The farm buildings at Bolts Walls have been demolished and replaced by unattractive sheds. Elsewhere, one circular and one rectilinear sheepfold, three old mine levels and a defunct TV relay station can be spotted - some of the green cable appears at one point on the left of the path! Just beyond the old corrugated iron shelter, see if you can find two or three large stones set into the ground with protruding wrought iron brackets - a relic of the old line.

The last cutting before Bolts Law is the deepest. Marvel at the effort. Continue to the buildings and find a grouse shooters' butt on the right, just beyond the summit. In the distance, the curving line continues and you are free to walk further if you wish.

RETURN DOWN THE TRACK, ABSORBING THE UNBROKEN VIEWS AND REMARKABLE INDUSTRIAL AND AGRICULTURAL ENDEAVOUR AROUND YOU.

The authors are natives of Rookhope and have village memories stretching over many years. Thomas Wall has lived there all his life. He comes from a mining family and has worked above and below ground in several Dale's mines, especially Stotfield Burn and Redburn. Peter Bowes, a former college lecturer, has done much research into the historical geography of Weardale from mediaeval times. He now lives at Stanhope.

Grateful thanks are due to the Rookhope Village Hall officials who have kindly granted public use of the car park. Parking is at the owner's risk.

Parties and groups are encouraged to use the hall by prior arrangement. Refreshments can be provided. Please contact either Marion Hogarth (01388) 517574 or Julie Lonsdale (01388) 517488

© Copyright on this publication resides with the authors and the North Pennines Heritage Trust. The Trust wishes to acknowledge the cooperation and financial assistance given by the Countryside Commission, Wear Valley District Council and the Norther Rock Building Society.

"Rookhope's Landscape Legacies" is published by the North Pennines Heritage Trust, 1995.

The North Pennines Heritage Trust

The North Pennines Heritage Trust works to conserve the historic remains of mans activities in the landscape of the North Pennines and to help people to understand and enjoy them.

Founded in 1987 the trust is a registered charity and limited company. From its base at Nenthead it carries out an expanding programme of conservation and interpretation.

So far it has opened for public access Smeatons famous waterwheel at Alston and has restored lime kilns at Middleton and Piercebridge and the fine chimney of the Gaunless smelt mill at Copley.

The Trust is currently restoring the famous Allendale Chimneys and the rare bingsteads at Hudgill. The Trust aims to start work soon on restoring the mineshop at Coldberry in the Hudeshope valley.

In 1997 The Trust will become the owner of the famous Lambley Viaduct over the South Tyne after it has been restored by British Rail.

The Trust's major project is the restoration and conversion of scheduled buildings at Rampgill to form 6 workshops and 2 offices for local businesses and the creation of a major visitor centre due to open in 1996. The Trust then plans to go on and to conserve the main features of this huge and facinating site and is planning for the eventual opening of one of the mines there to the public.

The Trust also publishes a series of booklets, of which this is the first, on interesting features of the North Pennines.

For members, the Trust publishes a newsletter four times each year and organises a programme of walks to interesting sites and a series of winter talks and events.

If you enjoy the North Pennines and would like to support our work, why not join the North Pennines Heritage Trust now?

Ring 01434 382037 or write to :

    The North Pennines Heritage Trust
    Rampgill Visitor Centre
    Nenthead
    Alston
    Cumbria
    CA9 3PD

Printed by Total Postweigh Ltd, Alston